IF EVER YOU GO TO DUBLIN TOWN

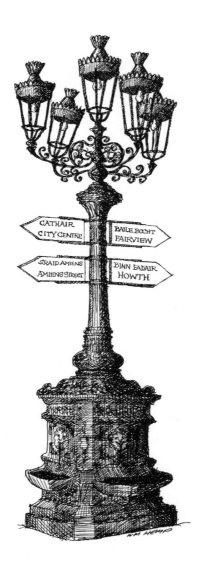

The Five Lamps -
A Dublin Landmark

Erected as a memorial to General Henry Hall, a native of Galway who served in the Indian Army. The Five Lamps represent the five Indian battles where Irishmen fell by the thousands.

if ever you go to dublin town

Written and Illustrated by

william hemp

The Devin-Adair Company

OLD GREENWICH

By the same author
New York Enclaves

Canadian Agent: Beaverbooks Ltd., Pickering, Ont.

ISBN 0-8159-6411-0
Library of Congress Catalog Card No. 77-92702

Printed in the United States of America.

For my mother Mary
and all the wonderful people
of Dublin

Acknowledgments

I want to express my appreciation to the Irish Tourist Board (Bord Fáilte), especially Sean Carberry and Patricia Tunison in New York and David Hanley in Dublin. My thanks also go to William Maxwell of Aer Lingus for his generous cooperation and the Consulate General of Ireland in New York for the use of their library.

While in Dublin I was welcomed by many cheerful individuals: Elizabeth Healy, editor of *Ireland of the Welcomes,* Billy Porter of Guinness's Brewery, Elgy Gillespie of the *Irish Times,* Muriel McCarthy of Marsh's Library, and, in particular, Brian Callinan, a gentleman and scholar, who introduced me to a myriad of Dublin's hidden treasures and whose mother extended her Irish hospitality.

I am indebted indeed to all the Dubliners who in their own personal way helped me in my research: the staff of Dublin's National Library, the double-decker bus drivers and conductors, the taxi drivers, the waiters in the pubs and the Garda in the streets, the storekeepers, the Jesuit priests in Belvedere College and the Trinity College students who had the kindness to stop and admire an artist's work.

A special thanks to the Coughlin family for the wonderful welcome they extended in Bray and Blackrock; to the Reverend Lawrence Fagan of St. Patrick's Church, Slane, who showed us the glories of the Irish countryside from Monasterboice to Trim Castle; to Sam Coe of the Wexford Historical Society; and to Michael O'Brien and his attentive staff at Ariel House in Ballsbridge.

My heartfelt appreciation goes to Anne Buckley Melvin for her invaluable aid in taking our children under her wing while my wife and I were in Ireland. Also a note of thanks to John McDonald Kane for his cheerful counsel, and to my mother, Mary Wendler Hemp, as well as my father- and mother-in-law, Walton and Margaret Collins, for their constant support.

Finally, a special tribute to my wife, Maggie, whose love for Ireland inspired the book in the first place, whose ideas shaped its direction, and whose many hours of research in the National Library provided so much invaluable information and historic data. Without her enthusiasm, encouragement, and everlasting love, this book could not have been completed.

Contents

St. Patrick arrived into a city noble in its people and favoured in its situation through the meeting of sea and river, rich in fish, famous for its commerce, charming on account of its verdant plains, built among oaken groves and surrounded by the haunts of wild beasts.

—Jocelinus de Brakelonda
(ca. 1182), *Life of St. Patrick*

Introduction

It has been pillaged and plundered, bombed and burned, but with an astonishing resilience has always bounced back and been rebuilt, richer and more rambunctious than before, yet somehow preserving something of all phases of its history, both tragic and glorious. This is Dublin, the ancient town the Greek geographer Ptolemy marked down on a map in A.D. 140 as Eblana, with an air of great antiquity permeating the medieval streets that meander about its two cathedrals; with charming echoes of the eighteenth century in the spacious, sunlit squares lined by handsome Georgian townhouses of mellow Bristol brick; with exuberant marketplaces alive with courtly, warm-hearted people, always smiling, always glad to see you. Now regarded as one of Europe's most beautiful, unhurried, and unspoiled capital cities, Dublin abounds in architectural treasures that transport the visitor back to bygone days. Strolling about the paved and cobbled streets, where the public signs are written in both Gaelic and English, is a journey into the past, an excursion into another era that gives the tingling sensation that the clock in the Custom House must have stopped ticking two hundred years ago.

If ever you go to Dublin Town, often called "The World's Largest Village," you will discover the narrow quays along the River Liffey that Sean O'Casey trod, still with their horses and drays; the tree-shaded canals with their towpaths and locks so vividly described by James Joyce in *Ulysses;* the lively markets where present-day Molly Malones chant their wares; the quiet cul-de-sacs lined by weathered townhouses haunted by the ghosts of such immortal Irish writers as Joseph Sheridan LeFanu, Oscar Wilde, Oliver St. John Gogarty, and William Butler Yeats.

There are so many districts of Dublin to disarm the "world-besotted traveler" one wonders where to begin: Trinity College, a classical complex of manicured lawns and Corinthian-columned temples, where Jonathan Swift and Edmund Burke and Oliver Goldsmith studied; Fitzwilliam Square, where Jack Yeats worked at his easel splashing bright colors on canvas. Dublin is steeped in history, and the list of legendary landmarks goes on from Guinness's Brewery and the Gaiety Theatre to Glasnevin Cemetery and grim Kilmainham Jail.

This book focuses on twenty-six nooks and crannies of vintage Dublin that have retained their down-to-earth character and Old World enchantment. Opening with St. Audoen's Arch, where the medieval, walled town once stood, it explores the neighborhood known as the "Liberties" and looks into such old haunts as the Brazen Head Inn, licensed in 1666, and the Stag's Head on Dame Court, one of the city's most popular pubs. It visits Marsh's Library, the oldest in the land, which snuggles in the shadow of St. Patrick's spire, and lingers in the "Long Room" of Trinity College Library over the celebrated *Book of Kells.* Finally, it journeys out to Phoenix Park, where lion cubs romp in the Zoological Gardens and deer browse among the woods.

This book is not intended as a guide to the Irish capital. It simply presents an artist's impression of a few of the priceless treasures of the town—some famous, some obscure—that I found especially fascinating.

WILLIAM HEMP

Point Lookout, Long Island, N.Y.

St. Audoen's Arch

Once upon a time a cartographer with an eye for detail dipped quill pen in ink and drew a picturesque map of the "Dubline" of 1610. It shows a seaport town snuggled on the south bank of the River Liffey, surrounded by stone walls interspersed here and there by towers and gateways. On the river, spanned by a single bridge, four sailing ships rest at anchor. Within the crenellated walls small houses with high-pitched roofs cluster about Christchurch Cathedral. At the southeast corner stands "The Castle," its rectangular keep protected by circular towers and enclosed by a curtain wall and a ditch. Henry II, the Norman ruler of England, whose occupation of Ireland had the approval of Pope Adrian IV, himself an Englishman, held court on this site in 1172 and granted the city of Dublin to the people of Bristol with the free customs and liberties of their native city. Thus began the tragic and turbulent history of British rule over Ireland.

Since Speed sketched his original map the medieval walls and towers have crumbled to dust, and Dublin town has spread out in all directions. Yet, despite universal destruction by battle or wrecking ball, a single remaining gate into the city, along with a fragment of the thick original wall, survives to this day on the south side of Cook Street. This is St. Audoen's Arch, built around 1275 and named for the Norman Bishop Ouen, patron saint of Rouen, France. When you walk under this ancient archway and climb the rusticated steps to High Street, main thoroughfare of the walled city during the Middle Ages, you are tracing the footsteps of those who had a hand in carving out the destiny of Dublin.

Over the succeeding centuries St. Audoen's Arch has served not only as a gateway but also as a market and meeting place. During the 1500's country butchers sold their mutton and beef to the shoppers who converged here on market day. Back then the gate was manned by a "Beadle," who kept strangers, dogs, and swine out of the city. The gatehouse was let to the Master of the Tanners in 1602, and the guild held meetings there until the mid-eighteenth century.

At the top of the steps leading from the Arch stands the shell of Old St. Audoen's, the last of Dublin's seven medieval parish churches still in its original building. Constructed by the Normans in the thirteenth century on the site of a Norse church founded in 650, the time-honored tower contains six bells, three of them cast in 1423, the oldest in Ireland. Inside the church is the lucky stone of great antiquity, a beautiful Norman font, and the elaborate tombs of Rowland Fitz Eustace, Baron Portlester, and his wife, dating from 1455.

Alfred the Dane, a wealthy landowner, returning from a pilgrimage to the Holy Land, entered Dublin by St. Audoen's Gate. As he walked through the Arch he was suddenly inspired to open a hospital in Dublin similar to the leper hospital of St. John's he had seen near St. Eithne's Gate in Jerusalem. Soon afterward, he and his wife gave up their worldly goods, joined a religious order, and opened that hospital, the second oldest in the world after the one in the Holy City. It flourished for many centuries and accomplished countless good works.

The Brazen Head

Turn back its old grandfather clock to 1666, the year Charles II granted licenses to all victualers, and you would find the Brazen Head a very busy place: the cobbled stable yard crowded with carriages and coaches, whinnying horses, barking dogs, and grooms going about their chores; all forty-three bedchambers booked solid by visitors from Drogheda and as far away as Donegal; the tavern on the ground floor serving up tankards of wine, mead, and porter to a mixture of travelers and townspeople. Situated next to the "Bridge of the Black Strangers," erected in 1210 and until 1670 the only bridge across the River Liffey, the Brazen Head was a welcome sign to the weary wayfarer after a long, bumpy journey.

The old clock has ticked away four centuries, but the Brazen Head still stands, proud of its heritage as Ireland's oldest inn. Mentioned in 1668 as "the inn in a recess to the rere of Bridge Street," this half-buried treasure of white stucco and black trim lies tucked away at the end of a dark tunnel leading from a low archway at No. 20 Lower Bridge Street. The present hotel is said to stand on the site of a much older inn beside a bridge made of bundles of brushwood laid across the Liffey that gave Dublin its Gaelic name, *Baile Atha Cliath* (the Town of the Hurdle Ford). According to legend, the Brazen Head drew its name from a "well-known red-headed girl of ill repute," who, peering out of a window to get a good look at the siege of Limerick, lost her head to a Williamite army cannonball.

Inside the narrow, dimly lit hallway is a rickety staircase with delicately carved banisters. On the landing leading to the bedchambers the Brazen Head's famous clock still chimes away the hours. Farther on down the dark corridor to the right is the barroom, low-ceilinged and reeking with the smell of stout.

If the tobacco-brown walls of the barroom had ears and a tongue, they could tell many a tale about the Irish revolutionaries who gathered here—in 1798, 1803, 1867, and 1916: Wolfe Tone, Lord Edward Fitzgerald, Robert Emmet, Daniel O'Connell, William O'Brien, Michael Collins. Emmet, whose impossible dream was to achieve the political separation of Ireland from England by the establishment of an Irish Republic, hid here in the inn when the malicious Major Sirr, well served by informers, was searching him out. He was hanged from a crudely constructed gallows on September 20, 1803.

Emmet's writing table is still where he left it in 1803, against a wall in a gloomy corner of the bar. A sad reminder of the famous speech he delivered from the dock, ending with the immortal words: "When my country takes her place among the nations of the earth, then, and not till then, let my epitaph be written." His body was never found. According to legend it lies buried in "Bull's Acre," the first of Dublin's cemeteries, near the Royal Hospital in Old Kilmainham. Wherever his final resting place, the spirit of young Robert Emmet lives on in the old Brazen Head.

Christchurch Cathedral

First built about 1038 by the Danes when Sitric was ruler of Dublin, rebuilt in 1172 by Richard de Clare, Norman Earl of Pembroke (known as "Strongbow"), this historic cathedral church at the top of Lord Edward Street is the oldest building in Dublin. A stroll through this magnificent structure, linked by a graceful covered bridge to the Synod House, sweeps the visitor back to May 24, 1487. On that day Lambert Simnel, the boy pretender, was crowned Edward VI, King of Ireland and England by his Geraldine supporters, with a golden crown taken from the statue of the Virgin Mary in St. Mary's Abbey. And here today the bishops of the Church of Ireland meet once a year under their primate.

The cathedral, which serves the Protestant Archdiocese of Dublin and Glendalough, is cruciform in shape, with a nave, transepts, chancel, and choir. A monument to Strongbow lies in the south aisle beneath pointed arches and chiseled columns and marks the final resting place of the Norman crusader. The original tomb, crushed in the sixteenth century when the walls collapsed, was replaced by the stone effigy of a recumbent knight in black chain armor brought from Drogheda and believed to have belonged to the Earl of Esmonde. Beside the fierce Norman leader reclines the diminutive statue of his son, cut off at the waist. According to a sad legend, Strongbow was so enraged at his young son for showing cowardice in battle against the hostile Irish tribesmen that he struck him in half with his powerful sword. Lodged within the walls of dark limestone is a metal case said to contain the heart of St. Laurence O'Toole, archbishop here from 1162 to 1180 and the patron saint of Dublin.

Christchurch Cathedral was in a state of ruin when Henry Roe, a distinguished citizen, commissioned a complete restoration in 1871. The oldest part of the building is the crypt, a ghostly cavern consisting of arches and huge foundation stones stretching the entire length of the church. Here you can see the candlesticks and tabernacle used in 1689, when mass was celebrated with James II in attendance. Making Ireland his battleground to regain his throne, "James the Worthless" was decisively defeated by the Protestant William of Orange ("King Billy") at the Battle of the Boyne in July, 1690. After that, Irish Catholics came under a fierce tyranny of penal law.

On April 13, 1742, in the now vanished Musick Hall not far from the cathedral, George Frederick Handel conducted from his harpsichord the first performance of his *Messiah*, with the choirs of both cathedrals, Christchurch and Swift's St. Patrick's, taking part. Handel, bored with London and "driven by the Goddess of Dullness to the Hibernian Shore," found Dublin to his liking and composed his masterpiece to "offer this generous and polished Nation something new." The *Dublin Journal* later reported: "The Sublime, the Grand and the Tender, adapted to the most elevated, majestic and moving Words, conspired to transport and charm the ravished Heart and Ear."

The Liberties

This ancient quarter of Dublin, where Molly Malone wheeled her barrow of "Cockles and Mussels," once stood outside the medieval walled town, and being therefore free of the jurisdiction of the Lord Mayor and Archbishop, became known as "The Liberties." Here, in the seventeenth century, came those skilled Huguenots like Jacquard de Lyon, fleeing persecution in France, to set up the weaving industry and construct their high–gabled houses along the valley of the River Poddle, called the Coombe. Until the early nineteenth century this neighborhood, where Quakers and Jews also settled, was traditionally the center of religious tolerance, as well as of Dublin's textile trade.

In the 1700's there could have been as many as 3,000 silk looms working in The Liberties to produce poplin, the finest in the world, and many thousands of workers busily engaged in other branches of textiles—linen, wool, cotton. Dublin's handlooms have now almost completely disappeared, and there is only Tailor's Hall on narrow Back Lane to remind us of the golden age of the ancient guilds.

Completed in 1706 to the design of Richard Mills, Tailor's Hall was the original headquarters of the Tailor's Guild of St. John the Baptist, instituted by charter in 1418. Beneath its sagging slate roof the guilds of barbers, saddlers, tanners, hosiers, and curriers also met. Boasting beautiful windows, antique bricks, and a thick, pedimented gate, it is one of the few structures in Dublin that survives from Queen Anne's reign and the only remaining guild hall. The Catholic Committee, better known as the "Back Lane Parliament," with Wolfe Tone, a Protestant lawyer and instigator of the United Irishmen movement, met here in December, 1792, to demand Catholic emancipation and plan a Union with Protestant Dissenters.

During his tenure as Dean of St. Patrick's, Jonathan Swift, "absolute monarch of The Liberties and King of the Mob," born on November 30, 1667, at No. 7 Hoey's Court, near St. Werburgh's Church, where William Penn, founder of Pennsylvania, also lived, wrote a diatribe on behalf of the weavers, objecting to the law laid down in 1699 prohibiting the export of Irish manufactures. Swift wrote: "Ireland is the only kingdom of which I ever heard or read, either in ancient or modern history, which was denied the liberty of exporting their native commodities and manufactures wherever they pleased." Though his protest went unheard, he persisted in his attempts to improve the appalling living and working conditions of his flock—"Burn everything from England but her coal!" The people of The Liberties showed their admiration for the Dean when, on his seventieth birthday, his mental and physical health in fast decline, they celebrated by lighting bonfires and tar barrels around the Deanery. While only a few fragments remain today of The Liberties, the streets that weave about Tailor's Hall are still the warp and woof of Dean Swift's Dublin.

Guinness's Brewery

One day in 1759 an enterprising young man by the name of Arthur Guinness, who had just acquired a nine-thousand-year lease on an abandoned brewery near the western entrance to the city, called St. James's Gate, accidentally burned the wort and hops, thus creating a rich, black brew. Chalking it up as a mistake, he gave the batch away to passersby. When they returned later for more of Guinness's "dark stuff," his fortune was made! Since then Guinness's has never stopped brewing its famous black stout, with the foamy white head, and in the process filling the neighborhood near the Liffey with delicious smells. Henry Grattan, the parliamentarian, declared it in 1782 to be "the nurse of the people, and entitled to every encouragement and exemption." By 1914 the St. James's Gate brewery, affectionately called "Uncle Arthur," had outlasted Dublin's three hundred other breweries to rank as a wonder of the world, exporting more than any other brewery anywhere.

Behind Guinness's elegant archway today the visitor finds a miniature town covering some fifty-nine acres with its own narrow-gauge railway, printing plant, and powerhouse. Old maltings and oaken vats within stately buildings flank such modern structures as a research laboratory and huge gleaming tanks. And still standing at No. 1 Thomas Street, is the "Dwelling House," which was included in the original lease and where Arthur Guinness and his family lived until 1855.

A landmark that can be seen for miles around is the old "smock" windmill, known as St. Patrick's Tower. Situated on the brewery's Thomas Street premises, it was apparently built in 1805. Crowning the 135-foot high tower is a copper cupola covered with a pale green patina that harmonizes with the domes of the Custom House and the Four Courts on the opposite bank of the Liffey. A weather-vane bearing the four-foot-high figure of Ireland's patron saint, mitre and crozier in hand, swings in the wind at the top. Although the old mill's sails have long since been dismantled, it is still used for conditioning ale.

Guinness makes its stout by natural processes from barley, hops, yeast, and spring water pumped in from County Kildare twenty-five miles away. The procedure remains relatively the same as it was when Arthur Guinness made his first "bucket of brew." From the golden fields of Irish malting barley the grain is transported by trucks to the maltser and then to the Guinness malt stores. After the malt has been "mashed," the "wort" is strained off to tanks and pumped into burnished coppers, where hops are added. The liquid passes through refrigerators along to the tuns for the most important process of all, fermenting, performed by the yeast. Next, the stout is stored for a specified period in vats—blended with loving care, refined, clarified, and tested until the experts are completely satisfied of its perfection. Finally it is "racked," or filled into tanks or casks, which are shipped throughout Ireland or loaded aboard Guinness's three specially designed motor vessels—*Grania, Gwendolyn,* and *Patricia*—for transport around the world.

St. Patrick's Close

One of the smallest streets in Dublin, St. Patrick's Close, where the lamp standards are festooned with shamrocks, takes pride in having as next-door neighbors the oldest public library and the largest church in Ireland: Marsh's Library and St. Patrick's Cathedral. These treasures evoke colorful memories of three immortals of Irish history—Saint Patrick, Archbishop Marsh, and Dean Swift.

The Library, founded in 1702 by the scholarly Narcissus Marsh, then Archbishop of Dublin, and designed by Sir William Robinson, provides a charming example of a seventeenth–century scholar's library and has the only surviving Queen Anne windows in Dublin. The gate opens into an herb garden alive with lavender and dotted with Michaelmas daisies. Black-and-white magpies bob about the inner quadrangle. The L-shaped interior, with magnificent dark oak bookcases decorated with carved gables topped by a bishop's mitre and three-wired alcoves or "cages," (where readers were once locked in with rare books to prevent pilferage), remains unchanged since the days of Dr. Elias Bouhereau, the Huguenot refugee who became its first librarian early in the eighteenth century.

The library contains some 25,000 volumes, mostly from the sixteenth, seventeenth, and early eighteenth centuries—liturgical works, missals, breviaries, and bibles printed in almost every language; books on medicine, law, science, travel, navigation and mathematics, as well as musical manuscripts, which were Marsh's pride and joy. One of the oldest books is Cicero's *Letters to His Friends*, printed in Milan and dating from 1472. Another rare item is a small book of Elizabethan poetry containing a poem to Queen Elizabeth by Sir Walter Raleigh, for some years a resident of Youghal, who introduced the New World potato to Ireland.

Farther down the crooked lane St. Patrick's granite spire, added soon after Swift's death, pierces the sky. Inside this 330-foot-long church, which serves as the national cathedral of the Church of Ireland, shafts of sunlight slant down on the wooden pulpit from which Swift preached. In the south aisle, where he once so feverishly paced, a polished brass plaque in the tile floor marks his grave and reads: "SWIFT Decan—1713 Obt. 19 Oct. 1745." A few feet away lies his "Stella" (Esther Johnson), immortalized in his journal. In the Gothic gloom you will discover a modest memorial to Turlough O'Carolan, the blind harpist composer and the last of the wandering Irish bards, who went from house to house on horseback composing songs for the families with whom he stayed.

The original church was built in 1191 outside the old city walls by Archbishop John Comyn on the site of the little wooden church of St. Patrick de Insula. Over the centuries the cathedral suffered much abuse, was twice ravaged by fire, and served as a stable for Oliver Cromwell's horses during his devastating "To Hell or Connacht" campaign through Ireland. Thanks to the generosity of Sir Benjamin Lee Guinness it was splendidly restored in 1864–69.

Dublin Castle

To walk around the upper and lower yards of Dublin Castle is to wrap yourself in the tightly woven political fabric of *Baile Atha Cliath*, as the Irish call their capital city. This two-level complex of brick, stone, and mortar on Cork Hill, behind the City Hall on Dame Street, was for almost seven centuries the symbol of England's occupation, as well as Ireland's center of government. Here Norse settlers, Norman knights, British viceroys, and Irish patriots built, fortified, ruled, and rebelled.

King John commanded in the early thirteenth century that a castle be built on the high ground where the Danes had erected an earth and timber fortress about A.D. 840 to guard the approach to the mud-and-wattle settlement in their day called Dyflin. The castle, with thick walls and circular towers at all four corners, was completed in 1220 and protected the Anglo-Norman vassals from the Celtic tribesmen who hid out in the Wicklow Hills. Surrounded by a curtain wall and ditch, it was impregnable to an enemy who might gain entry into the town. Later Queen Elizabeth ordered a residence constructed for her viceroys on the ruins of this stronghold. Today, after centuries of wars, political intrigues, long imprisonments, foreign rule, and rebel risings, the only fragment that remains of the medieval castle is the massive round Record Tower dating from 1205, which rises dark and forbidding at the southeast corner of the Lower Yard. Also known as the Black Tower, this three-story structure, with walls sixteen feet thick, holds the State Paper Office and is a repository for Ireland's historic documents.

Adjoining the Record Tower is the Catholic Church of the Most Holy Trinity, formerly the Chapel Royal, a jewel box of a building, begun by Francis Johnston in 1807. The gingerbread Gothic exterior is embellished with more than ninety heads carved by Edward Smyth, representing the sovereigns of England and other notables. The statue-heads of Brian Boru and St. Patrick guard the doorway on the east, while St. Peter and Dean Swift, once chaplain here, flank the north entrance. The interior is noted for the fan-tracery of plasterwork by George Stapleton, the pews and choir stalls of Irish oak, and the collection of viceregal names and coats-of-arms emblazoned on the stained glass windows, including that of Lord Cornwallis, who ruled here in 1798 after he surrendered to Washington at Yorktown.

In contrast to the atmosphere of melancholy in the Lower Yard, the Upper Yard reflects the spirit of the Georgian era, with its classical gateways and colonnaded apartments. Its best architectural feature is two great, triumphal-arch gateways flanking the Office of Arms (now the Genealogical Office and Heraldic Museum) with its charming Bedford Tower. On the south side of the Upper Yard stand the State Apartments, including the gold-and-white Presence Chamber, or Throne Room, and the impressively noble and ornate St. Patrick's Hall, now used for the installation of the President of Ireland at the beginning of his term of office.

Stag's Head Pub

Dublin public houses, like Dublin people, come in a variety of shapes and sizes. There's McDaid's, the "Poet's Pub" in Harry Street, where Borstal Boy Brendan Behan set up his typewriter and glass in the corner and worked on his plays, and where Patrick Kavanagh, another writer-in-residence, stopped in for a "jar." The Long Hall has an opulent bar crowded with bric-à-brac. Doheny and Nesbitt's, colorful and convivial, makes a friendly forum for university students. At Mulligan's in Poolbeg Street, a hangout for dockers, printers, and newspaper people, where gas lamps still flicker on old brown woodwork, you can poke a hole through the smoke in the backroom. Neary's bronze, arm-shaped lamps beckon the after-theatre crowd on Chatham Street to its Edwardian interior, where salads and smoked salmon are specialties of the house. Still, the nostalgic favorite of townspeople and travelers alike is the Stag's Head, which has been hiding away at Number 1 Dame Court since the 1890's.

To seek out this authentic watering spot, be on the lookout for a passageway off busy Dame Street, marked by a mosaic in the pavement bearing the image of an elk. Duck through to cobblestoned Dame Court, where you discover a Victorian bastion of red brick that looks like an oversized cuckoo clock, its bottle-glass windows winking a warm welcome. Once inside, you'll be caught up in the ambiance of polished wood, old leather, and the heady scent of porter. The mahogany bar running along the mirrored right wall boasts a red-speckled marble top quarried in Connemara, a brightly burnished brass clock resting on an onyx vase, and the busiest barmen, or "curates" as they are called, in all of Dublin. The proud head of a seven-point stag demands your attention from his vantage point above the bar.

It is in pubs like the Stag's Head where you'll discover that Dublin is a city dedicated to gregariousness and the desire to quench a desperate thirst. So unwind on one of the nut–brown leather banquettes, and the affable waiter will attend to your choice of refreshment, be it a "pint of plain," "100-year-old Power's," sherry drawn from an ancient cask of Amontillado, or Irish Coffee. Relax and gaze upon the stained-glass windows that surround you, each tinted in delicate shades of pink yellow, and green and spotlighting an alert stag leaping about his habitat of gold scrollwork interspersed with fruits and leaves.

Building up an appetite? The Stag's Head has a mouth-watering menu chalked up daily and simmering on the kitchen stove, sending out marvelous aromas—steak and kidney pie, boiled bacon and cabbage, lamb chops, and stew, each served with slices of oven-fresh soda bread.

Dublin pubs are closed between 2:30 and 3:30 P.M., but reopen promptly to continue as a social center and a place of refuge. Pubs like the Palace, the Pearl, the Lincoln Inn, Toner's, and O'Donaghue's are the meeting grounds where Dubliners can discuss everything from the state of Ireland to the state of their health. Dublin's pubs have an early closing hour, however, which may be inconveniencing to those used to the American equivalent.

Trinity College

When the College of the Holy and Undivided Trinity, chartered by Queen Elizabeth I for the banishment of "barbarism, tumults, and disorderly living," opened its doors to students on January 9, 1593, it stood well outside the walls of the city. Soon Dublin began to spread eastward, encompassing the campus but leaving it still a peaceful haven away from the busy world of commerce. Enter beneath the Palladian arch of the main gateway and you will be struck immediately by the quietude of Trinity's classical Parliament Square: velvet lawns of emerald green, twisted trees casting long shadows across Corinthian columns of gray granite and time-worn cobblestones that have felt the footsteps of such famous alumni as Oliver Goldsmith, Edmund Burke, and Jonathan Swift.

The centerpiece and crowning glory of Trinity's thirty-seven acres is the Campanile, encasing the great bell of the college. As you enter the square you will see on your right the Examination Hall, erected in 1787, and on the left its "twin," the Chapel, consecrated in 1798. The quadrangle to the east is Library Square, bounded on the south by Thomas Burgh's great library, which was opened in 1732 and now contains over a million books. Its famous "Long Room," seventy yards in length, one of the largest rooms in Europe, houses beneath its wooden barrel-vaulted ceiling, a collection of some of the finest illuminated Celtic manuscripts to be found anywhere on earth.

Each year well over a quarter of a million people visit the old library to look upon the *Book of Kells*, described as "the most beautiful book in the world." Completed around A.D. 800 when Ireland was known throughout Europe for its saints and scholars, four monk-artists, and maybe more, labored a lifetime in St. Columba's Monastery of Kells in County Meath to complete this Latin copy of the Gospels, the crowning achievement of Celtic art. The skins of a hundred and fifty calves were used to produce the smooth vellum leaves; the vibrant colors were pressed from local plants and flowers. Its imaginative ornamentation, its microscopic tracery, its floral and geometric motifs, including birds, dragons, and animals as well as human figures, have led antiquarians to believe that it must surely have been the work of angels rather than of men!

Among the library's collection of rare illuminated volumes are the *Book of Durrow*, the *Book of Leinster*, and the *Book of Armagh*. The Brian Boru Harp, which according to tradition belonged to the heroic High King of Ireland who was killed defeating the Danes at the Battle of Clontarf on Good Friday, 1014, is credited with being the oldest in existence.

The Rubrics is the oldest building on campus, dating from around 1700. The Provost's house, built in 1760, is considered the grandest Georgian house in Dublin still used for its original purpose. Students come from every corner of the world to study on Trinity's tranquil campus, an oasis of learning in the heart of Ireland's capital.

Today Trinity College Dublin (generally abbreviated as TCD) is renowned for its courses in Medicine, Science, and Engineering, as well as the Liberal Arts.

Kildare Street

Leinster House, the most splendid of Dublin's mansions, was built in 1745 on the south side of the Liffey for the twentieth Earl of Kildare of the Fitz-gerald family. Being so far out in the country, people thought it strange that he wanted to live on the wrong side of town. Lord Kildare's reply was: "Wherever I go, fashion will follow me." Time has proven him right. The classic Georgian residence designed by Richard Cassels, the German architect, now faces Kildare Street in the heart of the city, and has become the seat of the Dail Eireann, the Irish House of Parliament, flanked on the right by the National Museum and on the left by its twin, the National Library. Here John Fitzgerald Kennedy came on June 28, 1963, to address the Dail and receive the Freedom of the City of Dublin.

The National Museum to the right of Leinster House contains beneath its sky-lighted ceiling a fascinating collection of early antiquities, rich in design, skill, and aesthetic beauty, which tell us something of the glory of Ireland's past: cres-cent-shaped lunulae of beaten gold, worn by pagan kings and dating from 1800 B.C.; cauldrons of sheet bronze from around 700 B.C.; the Cross of Cong, made about 1123 to house a portion of the True Cross brought from Rome; wax writing tablets and parchments found in bogs.

The Tara Brooch, a work of sublime artistry, dates from the early eighth centu-ry. Found on the seashore at Bettystown near Drogheda, this ring brooch, fash-ioned of silver, heavily gilt, and gloriously inset and interlaced in copper overlaid with silver and gold filigree, is unique in that front and back are equally ornate in design. The Ardagh Chalice, a two-handed silver cup of the early eighth century found in a ring fort at Ardagh, is the finest surviving example of Irish metalwork of the Early Christian period. Encircled by a band of gold filigree offset by studs of red and blue glass, it is burnished with the names of the twelve apostles.

Across Leinster Yard stands the National Library of Ireland, holding over a half-million volumes and the most complete collection of old Irish newspapers in the world. In the warm mahogany reading room, beneath a dome banded by a Wedgwood blue frieze alive with plaster cupidons, readers and researchers can reap the benefits of its store of literary treasures. You will always be given helpful service by the efficient staff at the public service counter.

Running dead end into Leinster House is Molesworth Street, lined with an-tique shops and some of Dublin's oldest houses. Bernard Shaw worked four mis-erable years as a solicitor's clerk at Number 15. Nearby run the two other streets Oliver St. John Gogarty thought were the best in Dublin: Dawson Street, site of Mansion House, the traditional home since 1715 of Dublin's Lord Mayors, and Grafton Street, the city's most fashionable shopping district.

The Kildare Street Club at the corner of Nassau Street has been referred to as the last stronghold of the fading Ascendancy, otherwise known as the (largely Protestant) Anglo-Irish. These are the people of the Big Houses behind the walls, victims to a large extent of the 1921 Troubles. Today Desmond Guinness's Irish Georgian Society is preserving and restoring many of these seventeenth- and eighteenth-century mansions.

Gaiety Theatre

Mention the word theatre anywhere in Dublin and what's the first name that comes to mind? The Abbey Theatre, of course. And rightly so. For the world-renowned Abbey has been the focal point of the Irish National Theatre Society, founded in 1897 by William Butler Yeats, Lady Augusta Gregory, and Edward Martyn. An example of its impact on Ireland's history was during the Easter Rising of 1916, when by chance or design it was presenting Yeats's *Cathleen ni Houlihan*, a play picturing Ireland as an ageless woman for whom the young men leave their brides to die. Many feel the Abbey's performances had a significant inspirational effect on the national insurrection. It was on February 8, 1926, in the original 500-seat theatre (nicknamed "The Shabby") that Sean O'Casey's blazing masterpiece *The Plough and the Stars* opened, with Barry Fitzgerald playing the role of the boastful drunkard, Fluther Good. Dealing with Dublin tenement life during The Troubles, it literally started a riot with the first night audience by portraying the Irish not only as saints but sinners as well. So if you're searching for theatre steeped in the tradition and folklore of Ireland, the Abbey is the place to find it.

On the other hand, no visit to Dublin would be complete without booking tickets to a spirited show at the Gaiety, the oldest theatre in the city. This mid-Victorian landmark on South King Street, founded by the brothers John and Michael Gunn, opened on November 27, 1871, with the presentation of Oliver Goldsmith's *She Stoops to Conquer*. Since then the Gaiety has spotlighted so many stars and brought so many smiles to countless patrons that it is probably the most aptly named place in all of Dublin. Because of its policy of bringing visiting companies and artists to the city, the list of those who have played here from its earliest days is dazzling: Edwin Booth, Barry Sullivan, Henry Irving, Beerbohm Tree, Lily Langtry, Sarah Bernhardt, and other immortals. The first presentations of Shaw's work in his native city were seen at the Gaiety in 1907: *Caesar and Cleopatra*, and *Captain Brassbound's Conversion*, with Ellen Terry in the role of Lady Cicily.

The 1930's saw the introduction of the legendary O'Dea-O'Donovan partnership, with Harry O'Donovan writing the scripts and Jimmy O'Dea, a leprechaun-like man with big, sparkling eyes, becoming one of the most popular pantomimists ever to tread the Gaiety's boards. After their first production, *The Horse Show Revue*, the happy "O'D" combination was to enjoy many successful seasons and to make Dublin, "Biddy Mulligan," and the Gaiety synonymous. The 1950's introduced the diminutive figure of Maureen Potter, a dancer and singer with a great gift of comedy, who joined Jimmy O'Dea at the top of the Gaiety bills. In 1964 both starred in *Finian's Rainbow*, which was to be O'Dea's last stage appearance before his death the following January. His final song in that show ended: "We will meet in Gloccamorra . . . Some fine day. . . ."

Red plush seats, colored lights, two tiers of baroque balconies, the safety curtain painted with gaudy advertisements—this is the Gaiety.

St. Stephen's Green

Weeping willows cast golden-green reflections into an artificial lake. Meticulously tended beds of begonias grow beside a granite memorial arch. Young lovers, old soldiers, university students, mothers with babies in perambulators, and pretty girls on their lunch hours sun themselves on park benches or feed the ducks that paddle beneath a rustic bridge. These happy scenes of sunlight and shadow await the visitor to Stephen's Green, Europe's largest square and Dublin's oldest public pleasure garden, originally laid out in the 1660's.

Lining the outer edges of this oasis of flowers and trees in the heart of the city are modern art galleries, well-stocked bookstores, crowded restaurants, and ivy-covered mansions. Standing like a jeweled crown among them is the Shelbourne Hotel, a happy combination of garnet brick and pearl stucco, a living symbol of Dublin's hospitality, grandeur, and good life. As you step into the lobby of this internationally famous hostelry, you feel you've arrived.

The Shelbourne's history began in 1824 when four brick townhouses, standing side by side on the site of Lord Shelbourne's residence, were opened as a hotel by Martin Burke, a Tipperary man. William Makepeace Thackeray stayed there in 1843 and found it "a respectable old edifice much frequented by families from the country, and where the solitary traveler may likewise find society." In 1863, the Shelbourne was sold to new owners, who decided to tear down the old hotel and construct a majestic new one. Today the name "Shelbourne," inscribed in blue-and-white mosaic on the front strip of a glass awning, welcomes guests from all over the world who have heard that this is *the* place to stay when you are in Dublin. Four bronze-brown statues—two Nubian princesses and two slave girls, each holding a torch lamp—stand sentinel on the balustrade. Amid such Victorian splendors, visitors enjoy modern comforts with the elegance of a more leisured past.

After dinner in the Saddle Room or a drink at the busy Horse Shoe Bar, a stroll into Stephen's Green will introduce you to Dubliners at their evening best. Just across from the hotel is a monument to Theobald Wolfe Tone, leader of the United Irishmen in the Rising of 1798. After a fatal expedition to Bantry Bay, Tone cut his throat rather than be executed by the British. There are many other memorials to be seen within the twenty-two acres of the Green's open space: a bust of James Clarence Mangan, the poet; a monument to Countess Markievicz, who as second in command of the Citizens Army outpost in the Green during the 1916 Rebellion took part in the "Siege of the Shelbourne"; a block of Wicklow granite with a bronze plaque honoring O'Donovan Rossa, the Fenian leader, and Henry Moore's bronze memorial to the poet W. B. Yeats. Another name closely associated with the Green is that of Lord Ardilaun, who as Sir Arthur Guinness laid out and landscaped it at his own expense in 1880.

Ely Place

Once the haunt of many prominent Dubliners, the tranquil cul-de-sac called Ely Place echoes with memories of poets, patriots, prophets, and politicians out of Ireland's past. John Philpot Curran, orator and member of the Irish Bar, who violently disapproved of his daughter Sarah's involvement with the young rebel Robert Emmet, lived at Number 4. Later this became the home of George Moore, first of the modern Irish short story writers and a prolific novelist. His three-part memoirs, *Hail and Farewell*, tell of this neighborhood and describe the personalities of the Literary Revival he invited to glittering dinner parties held in the charming little garden across the street. Lord Clare, or "Black Jack" Fitzgibbon, as he was called, occupied Number 6. As Attorney General he was hated for having ordered the execution of the leaders of the 1798 Rising.

Handsome, erudite, and bawdy Oliver St. John Gogarty lived at Number 25 Ely Place, now the Royal Hibernian Academy. Famous as a surgeon, senator, writer, and wit, Gogarty caught the natural flavor of Dublin in his book of reminiscences, *As I Was Going Down Sackville Street*. James Joyce, whom he met while both were waiting for books at the National Library one night in 1903, modeled the "stately, plump Buck Mulligan" of *Ulysses* after Gogarty.

George William Russell, painter, poet, playwright, philosopher, economist, and editor, lived during his twenties at Number 3 Ely Place with a community of young Theosophists. A pantheistic worshiper of nature, he wrote under the pseudonym AE. The mystical Russell discovered and encouraged many a young writer, including Joyce, Padraic Colum, James Stephens, Frank O'Connor, and Austin Clarke.

Ely House, at Number 8, built for Henry Loftus, Marquess of Ely, by far the finest mansion in the cul-de-sac, faces down Hume Street into Stephen's Green. This splendid townhouse was built by Michael Stapleton in 1770 for the Marquess, a man of vast wealth and vivid imagination. It is noted especially for its sumptuous staircase, unique in Dublin, with a magnificently flamboyant balustrade and a life-size figure of Hercules carved in stone standing at its foot. The mansion now serves as headquarters of the Knights of Columbanus, who are happy to receive visitors provided you call at a reasonable hour.

Just north of Ely Place runs Merrion Street Upper, where, in Mornington House at Number 24, Arthur Wellesley, better known as the Duke of Wellington, was born in 1769. As a youth Wellington attended classes at Samuel Whyte's Academy at Numbers 78-79 Grafton Street, now the site of Bewley's Cafés Ltd., famous for exotic teas, fresh roasted coffees, and marvelous breads, cakes, and scones. For over a century shoppers and businessmen, artists and writers, have chatted across Bewley's marble-topped tables and munched on those light yeast cakes, speckled with currants, raisins, and sultanas, called "Barmbrack." The atmosphere in Bewley's is so merry and the aroma so delicious that every day seems like Christmas.

Merrion Square

Embracing a population of over half a million, Dublin can qualify as the most complete example of an eighteenth-century European capital in the world today. This is best exemplified by the dignified rows of Georgian houses that surround Merrion Square, with their sparrow-brown brick facades, russet vines, wrought-iron balconies, tall parlor windows, and torch stands. A walk through the second largest of Dublin's squares or a bicycle ride around it will treat you to Georgian streetscapes at their finest, as well as acquaint you with many of the great names in Ireland's history.

Sir William Wilde and his wife, the patriotic poetess who wrote for *The Nation* under the nom de plume "Speranza," lived a Bohemian life at Number 1 Merrion Square North in a huge gray corner house that glowed in perpetual candlelight. Sir William, surgeon-oculist to Queen Victoria, was also a serious archeologist and antiquarian and the father of Oscar Wilde, poet, playwright, and notorious wit. *The Importance of Being Earnest, The Picture of Dorian Gray*, and *The Ballad of Reading Gaol* are among Oscar's best-known works. Born in 1856 around the corner at Number 21 Westland Row, he was reared on Merrion Square in a sophisticated atmosphere of boisterous parties and sparkling conversation amid the wide circle of his parents' fascinating friends.

Daniel O'Connell, a Kerryman and brilliant lawyer, who fought for the passage of the Emancipation Act in 1829 giving Catholics the right to sit in Parliament, lived at Number 58. In 1841 O'Connell, known variously as the "Counselor," the "Liberator," "King of Ireland," and "King of Beggars," was elected the first Catholic Lord Mayor of Dublin since the seventeenth century. After his release from Richmond Prison, Ireland's great folk hero addressed a huge crowd of admirers from the balcony of his impressive home on the square.

During the 1920's, when he was a senator of the Irish Free State, William Butler Yeats, the dark, hypnotic-eyed Irish poet, playwright, and a Nobel Prize winner, lived at Number 82. Generally regarded as the greatest poet of his time, Yeats was the chief instigator, along with Lady Gregory, AE, and J.M. Synge, of the Irish Literary Renaissance, which produced a body of work unexcelled in the twentieth century. Deeply affected by the 1916 Easter Rising ("Did that play of mine send out Certain men the English shot?"), Yeats died in 1939 and is buried in Drumcliffe Churchyard "under bare Ben Bulben's head," Co. Sligo. His memorable epitaph reads: "Cast a cold eye/On life, on death./Horseman, pass by!"

On the west end of Merrion Square stands the National Gallery, with many superb paintings by the Old Masters, a comprehensive collection of Irish painting and sculpture, and an excellent restaurant. Works by all the most famous Irish artists are on exhibit here. Outside the gallery visitors are greeted by a sprightly statue of George Bernard Shaw. Born July 26, 1856, at Number 33 Synge Street on Dublin's south side, Shaw left a third of his estate to the gallery, where he said he learned more than he did at school.

Grand Canal

In the nineteenth century light barges towed by horses plied daily over Irish waterways between Dublin and the River Shannon carrying passengers at rates below those charged by the stagecoaches. Old prints in the city's museums and antique shops show that these roofed water buses looked like little Noah's arks decorated with gold leaf and bright paint, and, like their competitors on land, carried passengers both inside and out. If the going over the midland bogs was a bit on the slow side—four to six miles an hour at the most—it was a pleasure to glide across the "liquid roads," through the numerous locks, and enjoy the hearty meals that were served. Gone forever are these "flyboats," as they were called, but a stroll beneath the trees along the tranquil Grand Canal, with its bridges, locks, gates, and waterspills, brings an artist's sketch vividly to life.

Begin your promenade at the Mount Street Bridge, a sentimental spot considering that this was the scene of a battle during the 1916 Rising, when a small band of rebels held up a column of British troops for several days and inflicted heavy casualties. At Mount Street Upper you reach Huband Bridge, a rare treasure of historic Dublin, which leaps over the canal like a rainbow of stone. A quick glance at the graceful balustrade, the fine carvings, and the center tablet inscribed in 1791 is enough to explain why this is considered the most beautiful of the capital's few remaining unaltered canal bridges. Leave the towpath awhile, sit down on the grassy side bank, catch your breath, and listen. Listen to water spilling over locks . . . to churchbells ringing . . . to ships sounding their horns on the distant quays . . . to the chatter of children as they head for the park in Merrion Square.

Directly behind the Huband Bridge rises St. Stephen's Church, floating on an island of concrete in the middle of Mount Street Crescent. Nicknamed the "Pepper Canister" Church because of its peculiarly shaped clocktower belfry, St. Stephen's was designed in 1824 by John Bowden, who got his inspiration from the Greek temples on the Acropolis in Athens. Returning to the canal, you arrive at Mespil Road, where terraces of Georgian houses cast their reflections in the sluggish waters.

Overlooking the canal locks by the Baggott Street Bridge, where the satiric poet Patrick Kavanagh often sat, is the modern glass headquarters of the Irish Tourist Board, which operates under the Gaelic name *Bord Fáilte*, meaning "Board of Welcomes." Farther on to the right is Wilton Place, a quiet street harboring a row of Georgian residences. If you walk along the canal to the corner of Ranlegh Road, you will come to still another jewel of Georgian days, Portobello House, a grandiose building painted gray and white, with a charming clocktower. For many years it served as the Grand Canal Hotel, accommodating passengers who arrived in the city on the barges. Later it was converted into a nursing home. Here Ireland's prolific painter, Jack Yeats, spent his last years, gazing long hours from his window at the picturesque canal.

Dublin's two canals, the Royal, north of the Liffey, and the Grand, on the south, have captured the imagination of Irish writers.

Fitzwilliam Square

Dubliners derive a certain sense of identity and enjoy the feeling of continuity with the past provided by the familiar buildings surrounding them on all sides like palisades. This is especially true of Fitzwilliam Square, dating from 1820, the smallest and best preserved of the city's Georgian squares. Here the speckled bricks of the houses are so red, the stone steps so white, the brass knobs and plates upon the front doors so brightly shining that you are reminded of the paintings of Jack Yeats. Which isn't surprising, since that most original and imaginative modern painter of Irish scenes lived on the corner of the square at No. 19. A plaque on the tall house topped with towering chimneys reads: Jack B. Yeats lived and worked here. Painter 1871-1957. His brother was the poet.

Stroll about this delightful enclave and you will enjoy a feast for the eyes—the doors of Fitzwilliam Square, each offering a special morsel to please the passerby. One round-headed doorway in the Doric style may be painted a bright bottle-green. Another, framed by Ionic columns, may be Bristol blue. Others, with glazed sidelights, pop into the line of vision in bedazzling shades of burnt orange, Burgundy red, and buttercup yellow. Enormous fanlights of segmented leaded glass in delicately decorative designs, a motif invented by Palladio, shimmer overhead. Brass door knockers, each so highly polished you would think the Lord Mayor was expected to stop in, sparkle in the sunlight. Dublin door knockers come in all shapes and sizes: lions holding rings in their jaws; Greek goddesses with blossoms twined about their tresses; simple swags hanging from urns.

Jack Yeats, who spent his youth in County Sligo in the West of Ireland, began his career as an artist by sketching the tramps, tinkers, ballad singers, and sea captions of that region. Later, some of his best paintings were done during The Troubles and the bitter Black and Tan days: "Bachelor's Walk," "Communicating with Prisoners," and "The Funeral of Harry Boland" are notable. In time Yeats discovered color. With his palette knife thick with pigment he produced such masterpieces as "Tinker's Encampment," "The Salt Marshes," and "The Quiet Man." Some of Jack Yeats's greatest pictures were done after his eightieth year, and he stopped painting only two years before his death in 1957.

Sauntering about the major streets and squares of Dublin, your first impression is of grandeur and spaciousness, an open-air roominess that lets you bask in sunlight no matter which side of the street you may be walking on. For this we have to thank the "Commissioners for Making Wide and Convenient Streets." Established in 1757, Europe's first official town planning authority, the Commissioners had the breadth of view to create avenues that astonish by their width, such as Sackville Street, later renamed O'Connell Street, 154 feet wide, and Baggott Street, 100 feet wide. Roam the thoroughfares off Fitzwilliam Square, and you will well appreciate the successful results of the Commissioners' work—vast Georgian streetscapes with their vistas bounded by the River Liffey at one end and a distant glimpse of the cloud-shrouded Wicklow Hills at the other.

Ballsbridge

The green, white, and orange tricolor flutters from the pavilion steeple. Flower-bedecked boxes are filled with cheering spectators. Brass bands play in the well-tended gardens. Swift stallions leap over hedges and barriers with breathtaking precision. Equestrians parade in highly polished boots and well-cut breeches from Callaghan's on Dame Street. This is Dublin Horse Show Week. And it all happens at the Royal Dublin Society's showgrounds in Ballsbridge, a beautiful tree-shaded neighborhood that derives its name from a bridge over the River Dodder and also serves as headquarters for the Irish Hospitals Sweepstakes.

The Dublin Horse Show, a national institution held annually in August since 1868 and recognized as Ireland's greatest social event, draws up to 150,000 horse lovers and sportsmen to the country every year. Ireland has a long tradition in the breeding and training of the finest horses in the world. The Horse Show is the place to see them going through their paces in an atmosphere of excitement and elegance.

Two thousand incredibly beautiful horses, thoroughbred stallions, yearlings, brood mares and foals, hunters, Arabians, and Connemara ponies—the cream of the crop—are entered for the Show classes or are offered for sale in the blood-stock paddock. Prize money and many valuable cups, trophies, and ribbons are awarded. International Jumping Contests, sponsored by leading Irish industrialists, have been a thrilling feature since 1926. Each year, on the invitation of the Society, crack riders from many nations compete for the coveted awards. The team contest for the Aga Khan Trophy—The Nations Cup—takes place on Friday and the International Grand Prix of Ireland for the Irish Trophy on Sunday, amidst pageantry that cannot be surpassed at any show in the world.

During Horse Show Week a trade fair consisting of over two hundred stands is staged in the various halls. Here Irish products—implements for spinning and weaving, skins and hides, woolens, earthenware, damask and lace—are displayed, demonstrating the high standards Ireland's industry has achieved. For three days the Royal Horticultural Society of Ireland stages its summer show in the Tudor-timbered Pembroke Hall with a display of the finest flowers, fruits, and vegetables the country can produce. Evenings Hunt Balls and champagne receptions are held. The hotels are packed, and reservations should be made well in advance for the occasion.

On June 25, 1731, fourteen men concerned about improving the condition of their country, especially its agriculture, met in Trinity College and formed the Royal Dublin Society for "improving Husbandry, Manufactures, and other useful arts." In 1815 Leinster House became its headquarters and remained so for 108 years. In 1880 fifteen acres were acquired in Ballsbridge. In 1924 the R.D.S. moved there in its entirety, and today the premises cover an area of about sixty-five acres.

Sandymount

Just a short ride by double-decker bus from the heart of Dublin, past rows of single-story terraces, lies the seaside suburb of Sandymount, the perfect spot for a picnic or a walk along a great stretch of strand. The bus will drop you off at the town's triangular green, surrounded by a cast-iron fence, shaded by palms, and furnished with inviting park benches, where you can sit and admire a handsome bust of Yeats the poet, born June 13, 1865, several blocks away at No. 2 Georgeville.

The Sandymount Stores, situated on the north side of the green, with its curved glass corners and delicately carved Victorian woodwork, is a rare jewel of the Irish shop tradition and a joy to visit. Trimmed in a rich shade of chocolate, the inner panels painted butter yellow, the chandler and the hardware temptingly invite you in to inspect their merchandise. The emporium is so small one wonders how it could possibly have supplied the needs of the citizens of Sandymount. Nonetheless, it has succeeded in doing just that for well over a hundred years, selling everything from spades and seeds to buckets and washing soda. Behind the well-worn wooden counter, with its polished scale and ancient cash register, the storekeeper greets you like an old acquaintance. The policy here has always been to offer personal service. So if it's one nail you need, that's what you'll get!

Around the corner in the shops strewn along Sandymount Road you can purchase a bottle of Spanish wine, a delectable Welsh pastry, a crisp apple or two for a picnic on the Strand, where the tide goes out so far one wonders if it will ever come back again. But before you do, visit Our Lady Star of the Sea Church. James Joyce mentioned this graceful edifice in *Dubliners*. Since he wrote that particular episode in the early 1900's, many a bridal pair have waltzed out of the chapel door into Sandymount's salty air to the music of mewing gulls.

Heading for Sandymount Strand, you will pass by row after row of solid brick and terra cotta villas in the late Victorian style peering out at Dublin Bay from behind monkey-puzzle trees. Across the way broods an abandoned Martello Tower, where, according to legend, smugglers were imprisoned in the extensive cellars below. Early in the 1800's many circular fortresses, exactly like this one, were built around the coast of Ireland because the British feared a Napoleonic invasion. Modeled after a prototype in Martello Bay, Corsica, erected by order of George III, and constructed of hewn granite with walls nine feet thick, these squat towers can still be seen from Howth down to Cork and up to Galway Bay.

Joyce lodged for awhile in No. 11 Martello Tower at Sandycove on the southern shore of Dublin Bay near the "Forty Foot" swimming cliff. Oliver Gogarty had become the tenant of the tower at the time at a yearly rental of eight pounds. The living room of the tower was opened as a repository of Joyceana in 1962 by Sylvia Beach, his publisher. It contains his first editions, manuscripts, walking stick, death mask, and the official receipt for the rent of the tower overlooking the breakers of the Irish sea.

River Liffey

The green-brown waters of the Liffey spring forth from the peat bogs of the Wicklow Hills and meander some seventy miles past great country houses like Castletown before flowing gently through the center of Dublin beneath gliding seagulls and a cobweb of busy bridges. The river, which gave the city its name, Dubh Linn, or Dark Pool, divides the Irish capital to the north and to the south. By far the best vantage point from which to enjoy the colorful panorama of the Liffey quaysides, with their mixture of bookstores, cloth merchants, and antique shops, is the "Ha'penny Bridge." Built in 1816 as the Wellington Bridge, it got the nickname from the halfpenny toll exacted many years ago to cross the river at this convenient spot.

Start from the north end of the bridge, where the Dublin Woolen Company has been dealing in Donegal tweeds and Aran Island sweaters since 1888, and walk west to Ormand Quay. Here you will come upon the Palladian façade of the Four Courts, the Irish Courts of Justice, casting its reflection in the river. Completed in 1796, it originally housed the courts of the King's Bench, Chancery, Exchequer, and Common Pleas. During the 1922 Civil War Pro-Treaty forces under Michael Collins demolished this magnificient structure with its massive green saucer dome after Anti-Treaty forces under Rory O'Connor had seized the building. It has now been restored to its former glory.

Retrace your steps now and head east past the open secondhand bookstalls on Bachelor's Walk to O'Connell Bridge, noted for being as wide as it is long. Named for "The Liberator," his statue guards the entrance into hurly-burly O'Connell Street, Dublin's widest thoroughfare. One block north on the left is the bullet-scarred General Post Office, where on Easter Monday, April 24, 1916, Padraic Pearse, President of the Provisional Government, issued the proclamation declaring "the right of the people of Ireland to the ownership of Ireland." Pearse and his outnumbered army of Irish Republicans made the G.P.O. their headquarters, but were bombed out by the British gunboat *Helga* anchored in the river. In the main hall stands the bronze statue of the dying Cuchulainn, Irish mythical hero, as a memorial to the sixteen leaders of the Rising executed by British firing squads.

Several blocks further east on the north quay of the Liffey is the Custom House, Dublin's pride and joy, built between 1781 and 1791 from the designs of James Gandon, an English architect of Huguenot parentage. Notable features of this architectural masterpiece are the fourteen colossal heads in the keystones of the arches on the main floor. Sculpted by Edward Smyth, they symbolize the Atlantic Ocean and the principal rivers of Ireland.

With its thirteen rivers, Ireland is a land linked romantically to the sea. Irish legend claims that St. Brendan the Navigator, a monk who founded a monastery at Tralee in County Kerry, sailed in a leather currach to North America about A.D. 550 in search of new peoples to convert.

Moore Street Market

"Go down to Moore Street and get your nose educated," said the Dublin comedian Jimmy O'Dea. Good advice for someone who wants to hear the thick brogues and catch the lilting conversations of Dublin. Yes, the open-air Moore Street Market, crowded with carts, spilling over with a wondrous variety of merchandise, exploding with vendors and visitors, is the place to go. Here you can listen to the "Me Jewel-and-darlin' " ladies of Dublin hoarsely hawking their fruits and vegetables—"Hey luv, bananas only fifty pence a bunch. T-anks, luv. Ta-ta!"

You will find this motley carnival around the corner from the G.P.O. on O'Connell Street and just off Henry Street. The gaudy shop fronts have a certain country charm and a human scale about them, with their adventurous use of color on the façades and their facia boards hand painted to give a three-dimensional effect. Even if you don't intend to buy a thing, a stroll down Moore Street, with a stop at Madigan's for a quick "pint," is a fascinating excursion in terms of people-watching.

Browse about the open-air stalls with their pyramids of vegetables and fruits. Hear the rumble of drays and the clip-clop of horseshoes hitting freshly-hosed cobblestones. Savor the briny fragrance of fresh-caught fish, including mackerel, cod, plaice, Galway oysters, and those delicious Dublin Bay prawns. Peer into a butcher shop window and see rabbits, geese, turkeys, lambs, and Irish bacon in seemingly endless variety.

Dubliners will tell you that it's a tradition in Moore Street for the black-shawled mothers who have worked here all their lives to pass on their "businesses" to their comely daughters. There is even a "queen" of the marketplace, and "Rosie" has reigned for many years. Get there at dawn and meet these modern-day Molly Malones, with wit and wisdom at their very fingertips, as they smoke and snack on sandwiches before the crowds arrive. Chat with them as you make your way through the market stalls, and you will readily understand why Dubliners are considered the most warmhearted, affectionate, loquacious people on earth.

A short trek north from the market takes you to two relics of old Dublin. In a blind alley called Meeting House Lane off Mary's Abbey you'll discover what remains of the ancient Chapter House of the Cistercian Abbey of St. Mary, founded in 1139. In the 45-foot-long, vaulted Council Chamber, now the basement of a warehouse, in 1534 "Silken" Thomas, the Geraldine, flung down the Sword of State he held as Henry VIII's Lord Deputy and declared war against the Crown. He later paid for this gesture with his life. Climbing to the top of steep Henrietta Street, past dilapidated Georgian townhouses where old nobility of Dublin once lived, you'll bump into the back of an imposing granite building with bull's-eye windows and a huge gateway. This is the King's Inns, designed by James Gandon in 1795 as the Irish Inns of Court, with a library containing over 100,000 books. Here students for the bar sit for examinations, and dine in commons.

Parnell Square

He was the son of an American mother, whose father, the naval hero Charles Stewart, commanded the *Constitution* during the War of 1812, a country squire, and a strong Protestant. Everyone from wealthy Dublin spinsters to Connemara sharecroppers called him "The Chief." As President of the Land League he proposed many relief bills to help the Irish farmers, all of which were defeated by the British Parliament. Accused of condoning the Phoenix Park murders of Lord Frederick Cavendish and T. H. Burke by a secret group called "The Invincibles," he cleared himself and continued to lead the Home Rule Party with great success until his affair with Kitty O'Shea, revealed in a divorce case, brought him down from power. His name was Charles Stewart Parnell, dubbed "The Blackbeard of Avondale" by ballad singers—an elegant, full-bearded, fearless but tragic figure, for whom the largest square on Dublin's north side is named.

Charlemont House, on the north side of the square overlooking the Garden of Remembrance, a 1966 memorial to all those who died for Ireland in the long struggle for national independence, is the most important townhouse on the square. It was designed by Sir William Chambers as the Dublin residence of James Caulfield, the "Volunteer" Earl of Charlemont, a great patron of the arts, who supervised every detail while it was being built in 1762. Taking his seat in the House of Lords in 1754 at the age of twenty-six, the Earl later became Commander-in-Chief of the Irish Volunteers. In 1870 Charlemont House was sold to the Government; in 1930 it became the Municipal Gallery of Modern Art.

Several blocks west of the square, in the middle of St. Mary's Place, the needlelike spire of what is commonly called in Dublin "The Black Church" points a firm finger to the sky. Designed by John Semple and built of black Dublin stone in 1830 to be the Chapel-of-Ease, it is no longer a church. Richard Brinsley Sheridan, brilliant author of *The School for Scandal*, was born in 1751 around the corner at No. 12 Upper Dorset Street, and Sean O'Casey, the playwright, at No. 85.

On the square's south side rises the Rotunda Hospital, the second oldest maternity hospital in the world, founded in 1745 by Bartholomew Mosse, an idealistic doctor, appalled by the miserable conditions in which the poor women of Dublin had to give birth to their children. Its Rotunda Chapel, reached at the top of an exquisite staircase, is a jewel of old Dublin. Next to the hospital are the Rotunda Round Rooms, birthplace of the Irish Volunteers as well as the Sinn Fein organization, and the Dublin Gate Theatre, where Michael MacLiammoir and Hilton Edwards made theatrical history.

Closing Parnell Square at the top of O'Connell Street is the torch-topped monument made of Galway granite to "The Uncrowned King of Ireland." The statue by Augustus Saint-Gaudens at its base permanently casts in bronze Parnell's curious habit of wearing two overcoats at the same time. "The Chief" died October 16, 1891, at forty-five, of a broken heart in the arms of his wife, Kitty O'Shea. With him went out a bright light of hope for the poor people of Ireland.

Eccles Street

Frustrated by Irish provinciality and politics, a defiant, stubborn James Joyce departed from Dublin in 1904 at the age of twenty-two to live and write on the Continent. Yet many years later the artist-in-exile could close his nearsighted, pale blue eyes and with a passion for detail describe every shop front, signpost, and public house on any given street or square in the city. He committed the mind, the fabric, and the very spirit of Dublin to posterity when he wrote his epic novel *Ulysses*, published in Paris in 1922.

A journey to Eccles Street today, named for Sir John Eccles, Lord Mayor of Dublin in 1716, brings the immortal pages of Joyce's book immediately to life. Alas, Bloom's modest three-story house is just a burned-out shell, the roof having fallen in and the upper floors demolished in 1967. But the original front door has been removed to the safety of The Bailey, a pub in Duke Street just across from Davy Byrne's, the "moral pub" of *Ulysses*, where Bloom had his seven-penny lunch of "feety" green cheese and burgundy. On Bloom's dilapidated front stoop a few bright blossoms spring up between the cracks in the concrete as a reminder of Leopold and the earthy Molly, two fictional characters who demonstrated in print that Joyce knew the Irish people better than they knew themselves.

Farther down the street of tumbling tenements, in a crescent closing three vistas on Hardwicke Place, you find Dublin's finest and most elegant church—Great St. George's. Dating from 1802 and the work of the prolific Irish-born architect, Francis Johnston, who lived at No. 64, the 200-foot-tall spire and clocktower, which houses the "loud, dark iron bells" that Bloom used to keep track of the time, can be seen all over the city. It was in this church that the Duke of Wellington married Catherine Packenham on April 10, 1806.

Decorating nearby Great Denmark Street is Belvedere College, where Joyce was "steeled in the school of old Aquinas." Here from 1893 to 1898 he gathered most of the background material for his autobiographical novel *Portrait of the Artist as a Young Man*, which introduced his fictional creation, Stephen Dedalus. The Georgian building, originally known as Belvedere House, was constructed as a rural retreat from the central city for Colonel William Rochfort, 2nd Earl of Belvedere, in 1775. It enjoys one of the most dominating sites of all the great houses of Dublin, facing down North Great George's Street toward Gandon's glorious Custom House. Michael Stapleton, the stuccodore, lavishly decorated the Apollo, Venus, and Diana rooms with medallions of cupids and garlands of flowers.

When James Joyce left for Europe in 1904 he took with him a tall, young, auburn-haired girl from Galway with whom he was having an affair. Her name was Nora Barnacle. She became his constant companion, and they were finally married twenty years later. It was in Paris, Trieste, and Zurich that Joyce created *Ulysses*. Today, what remains of the house at No. 7 Eccles Street stands as a landmark to the Dublin exile, who died in Zurich in 1941.

47

Mountjoy Square

When Charles Dickens visited Dublin for a public reading and strolled the hilly streets north of the Liffey, he might very well have been inspired to write a tale about Mountjoy Square. His cast of characters would include, on the one hand, the family of Luke Gardiner, Lord Mountjoy, banker, landowner, and leader of the Crown's soldiers against the rebels of 1798, who so imaginatively laid out the Georgian square in 1789, and on the other, the poverty-stricken people living in misery just a stone's throw away in the worst slums of Europe.

During its Golden Age in the latter half of the eighteenth century Dublin glittered. Painters, architects, smiths, stucco experts, and designers of every kind came from abroad to set up their shops or studios and build Georgian townhouses for the leading intellectual lights on the long straight streets that led off the airy uphill squares. Michael Stapleton, the architect, built and decorated No. 1 Mountjoy Square for himself in 1791. With its superb central gardens, the square served as a Palladian backdrop for a vivacious society. Suddenly, with the Act of Union in January, 1801, which abolished the Irish Parliament, life in Dublin took on a new turn. Aristocratic families left for London, taking their money with them. Many of the rows of townhouses deteriorated into dilapidated tenements.

What happened in the Irish potato fields during the years 1842–45 didn't help to improve the prospects of the people who lived around Mountjoy Square. "The Great Famine" fell across the land like a chilling shadow. Caused by a blight that appeared on potato plants in various parts of Europe, it hit Ireland the hardest because her people depended entirely upon this one crop for their subsistence. Dublin became a huge camp for starving refugees from the countryside, and soup kitchens were set up. Two-and-a-half million people died of starvation, and women with children at their bosoms gnawed grass on all fours by the roadsides. The catastrophe forced hundreds of thousands to emigrate to America. Over fifty thousand peasants were evicted from their thatched-roof cottages when they couldn't pay their rent. The dwellings were then burned to the ground.

Today, Mountjoy Square symbolizes Ireland's plight over the centuries—her struggle to survive, the splintering of families, the oppression. Recently there has been a drive to restore this once noble neighborhood to its former glory. The house at No. 50 on the south side, now propped up with wooden stanchions, is being preserved by the Irish Georgian Society. On the north side a townhouse, built in the Adam style of repeating patterns, has been restored and decorated by a company of wine merchants. No. 39, which serves as a youth hostel, still possesses its classic simplicity.

The beauty of the houses surrounding Mountjoy Square lies not only in their tall parlor floor windows, their decorative fanlights, and their picturesque chimney pots, but also in their Dickensian character. Over the centuries the wind and the rain and the salty air from the Irish Sea have mellowed their brick facades and given them a melancholy air of faded glory.

Kilmainham Jail

Serpents, carved in stone and coiled for the strike, slither over the forbidding front gate. Skylights running along the rooftop illuminate the gloomy depths, containing spooky corridors and cellblocks haunted with the spirits of slaughtered heroes. Stout bars partially blind the windows that overlook the empty stonebreakers' yard, once filled with political prisoners. Thorny vines make a valiant attempt at climbing to the top of ramparts steep as the Cliffs of Moher. This is Kilmainham Jail, a hulking horror of gray granite built in 1796 by Sir John Trail, the Sheriff for County Dublin, and the brutal symbol of British oppression in Ireland. It serves today, worn and weathered, as an enormous monument to the procession of patriots who gave and risked their lives that Ireland might be free.

From the 1798 Rebellion came Napper Tandy, Henry McCracken, Wolfe Tone, and Thomas Addis Emmet, whose brother Robert was to be a prisoner here five years later. Others were the Sheares Brothers, John and Henry, two Republican barristers summarily executed for their association with the United Irishmen and buried in St. Michans family vaults. William Smith O'Brien, leader of the Young Ireland Party, responsible for the Rising of 1848, spent time in this dreary dungeon. He was followed in 1867 by the participants in the legendary rising of the Fenians under their hero O'Donovan Rossa. In 1881 Charles Stewart Parnell was incarcerated here. Parnell had sailed to America to get sympathy and funds for the farmers who toiled in cabbage patches and potato fields to pay the rent on their lands. Arrested upon his return on a charge of conspiracy, Parnell negotiated from his cell the Kilmainham Treaty with Britain's Prime Minister William Gladstone.

Padraic H. Pearse, the Dublin-born Gaelic poet, playwright, and headmaster of St. Enda's College, who led the Easter Week Rebellion in 1916, spent his last days in Kilmainham Jail. As Commander General of the Irish Republican forces, Pearse had said: "When I was a child of ten I went down on my knees by my bedside one night and promised God that I should devote my life to an effort to free my country. I have kept that promise." At thirty-seven he was shot at dawn in the bleak prison yard. James Connolly, union organizer and commandant of the Irish Citizen Army and second in command of the Post Office, was shot seated in a chair because his gangrened legs could not hold him up. Eamon de Valera, the last of the Revolutionaries to surrender, escaped execution by a hair's breadth because he was American by birth.

In 1924 Kilmainham Jail was closed for good. Falling into ruins, the prison was restored by voluntary workers as a historic museum and national monument and was reopened by President de Valera on Easter Sunday, 1966, fifty years after the historic event at the Post Office.

Glasnevin Cemetery

Aplace of peace sacred to the dead." These were the words Padraic Pearse used to describe Prospect Cemetery, Dublin's main burial ground, which most people call Glasnevin because of its location in that northwestern suburb beyond the Royal Canal and next to the Botanic Gardens. It is well worth the journey out Finglas Road just to walk along the mossy avenues of swaying cypress trees past stone angels, broken pillars, high crosses, family vaults, and the striking monuments that mark the graves of Ireland's illustrious patriots who once walked Dublin streets—O'Connell, Rossa, Parnell, Collins, and De Valera.

Entering Glasnevin by the main gate you come to a giant replica of an ancient Irish round tower of the type seen in the wooded valley of Glendalough. These belfries once served as lookout points and places of refuge for the monks between A.D. 850 and 1000, when Norse marauders arriving in longships harassed their Christian monasteries, centers of Celtic learning during the Dark Ages. This particular tower is the monument to Daniel O'Connell, the flamboyant statesman and florid orator. A short distance away rests a granite boulder with PARNELL chiseled in big letters, for though Charles Stewart Parnell was a Protestant, he was granted a ceremonial burial in this Catholic cemetery.

Glasnevin is also the resting place of Michael Collins, the stocky, square-jawed general, who at thirty-two was the driving force of the Revolution. Collins was killed during the 1922 Civil War when his convoy of military vehicles was ambushed in County Cork. Nearby lies Countess Markievicz, the former Constance Gore-Booth, who was nearly executed in 1916 for her part in the Easter Rebellion. O'Donovan Rossa, hero of the legendary Rising of the Fenians in 1867, who had suffered and languished many years in English prisons, died in America in 1915. His body was brought back to Dublin for burial, and thousands accompanied the hearse to Glasnevin. In his famous funeral eulogy at the graveside, Padraic Pearse exhorted his countrymen to resist British domination: "They have left us our Fenian dead and while Ireland holds these graves, Ireland unfree shall never be at peace."

Eamon De Valera, President of Ireland from 1959 to 1973, is buried in Glasnevin beside his wife Sinead. Born in New York City, the son of a Spanish musician and Kate Coll, an Irish immigrant from County Limerick, De Valera served his country in turn as mathematics teacher, revolutionary, President of the first Dail, Opposition Leader, Taoiseach, and finally President. He died August 29, 1975, his life having spanned almost a century of Irish politics.

John Kavanagh, dealer in "Wine and Spirits," at No. 1 Prospect Square, next to the back gate into the cemetery and in business since 1833, is one of the best-preserved examples of the traditional Irish pub, doors swinging into small cubicles with sawdust on the floor. Here, decade after decade, grave diggers have come to quench their thirst after a long day's labor.

53

Phoenix Park

New Yorkers treasure Central Park, Parisians have the Bois de Boulogne, Londoners their Hyde Park. But none of these can lay claim to a breathing space the likes of Phoenix Park, which looks from the air like an emerald-green welcome mat on the doorstep of Dublin. In this terrain of 1,760 acres measuring about seven miles in circumference Dubliners of all ages have romped and relaxed, played football, cricket, and polo since 1747, when the Royal Deer Park was thrown open to the public by the Earl of Chesterfield, viceroy at that time.

Phoenix Park's name comes from *Fionn Uisage*, which is Gaelic for "clear water," after a spring of mineral water near the north end of the Zoological Gardens. It was anglicized to the name of the bird rising from its own ashes, which you see on top of the column that stands beside the central drive through the park. This magnificent main avenue runs for nearly three miles through verdant lawns planted with fine chestnuts, majestic oaks, groves of hawthorn, and slender white birches. A herd of fallow deer roams at will through the fields and woods. From the park, where race horses gallop around the "Fifteen Acres" in the early morn, one is treated to a magnificent view of the Dublin skyline, accented by church steeples and copper domes.

Other points of interest in Phoenix Park are the Wellington Memorial, a 200-foot-tall obelisk that can be seen as far away as the Liffey quays, the People's Garden, the Zoo, the Magazine Fort, the Racecourse, the U.S. Ambassador's mansion, the Papal Nuncio's residence, and the residence of the President of Ireland. This dazzling white mansion was built by the park ranger Nathaniel Clements in 1757. It became the Viceregal Lodge a few years later, and in 1816 was greatly enlarged by the architect Francis Johnston, who added the south portico.

The Zoological Gardens, third oldest in the world after Paris and London, comprising thirty acres of the park, opened in 1831 with just one wild boar. It now offers a large and varied collection of animals and birds. Noted for breeding the first lion cubs in captivity, zoo records show that over six hundred honey-colored cubs have been born here since 1857. No one seems to know the zoo's secret, but lions just happen to love Dublin. In the exquisitely landscaped gardens surrounding a pond as smooth and shiny as a well-polished mirror, you can catch a glimpse of peacocks, crowned cranes, pelicans, and flamingos showing off their colorful plumage. And for the young-in-heart what could be more fun than a cageful of noisy chimpanzees or a ride on the back of an elephant?

At the entrance to the zoo stands a picturesque little cottage, the original gatehouse, which has remained unchanged since it was built in 1833 by Decimus Burton. Traditionally, gatehouses have given Irish architects a tempting opportunity to display their talents. This one, a whimsical interpretation of the thatched-roof cottage, is no exception. It has been embellished with dark oak timbers, brightened by leaded glass windows, and topped off with an intricately woven thatch. A delight to the eye, it makes an ideal entrance to a menagerie.